YouTul Growth Hack

Gain Free YouTube Subscribers by Scanning the Above Code!

All Rights Reserved
Copyright of Jake Radford

Preface

Hello,

I'm Jake Radford. My experience with YouTube has been truly transformative. While many relish the spotlight, my true passion is behind the scenes, cultivating YouTube channels, especially those that are faceless. The ever-changing and sometimes unpredictable YouTube algorithm has been my focus. I've studied its patterns, learning to adapt and pivot as needed. One of the most fulfilling aspects has been taking niche topics, which might seem to have a limited audience due to their niche nature and seeing them thrive and become profitably monetized in as little as 28 days. This success underscores the idea that with the right strategies, growth can be sustained and continuous.

If you're reading this, you might see a bit of your own curiosity and ambition reflected in my earlier days - a person with an idea, seeking the knowledge to bring it to life. I aim to provide that knowledge. But a word of caution: achieving this dream requires more than just enthusiasm. It calls for dedication, hard work, and a commitment to continuous learning.

Every chapter, every section of this book, is essential. I encourage you: read thoroughly, absorb the information. Achieving success, especially when there's potential financial reward, isn't always straightforward. However, by investing in this book, you've made a significant move in the right direction. It's worth noting that the insights here are based on the YouTube algorithm as it was at the time of writing. While the online world is fluid and ever-evolving, the core principles shared remain crucial.

I'm here to assist, to help you flourish and evolve. Initial growth might be slow. Your early 20-30 videos might not gain traction immediately. But that's perfectly fine. These initial efforts are foundational, helping you build confidence, acquire skills, and hone your approach. Strive to improve with each video, and over time, you'll see a marked difference in both your content quality and audience engagement.

Pursuing success on YouTube is no easy feat. There will be hurdles, moments of uncertainty, and periods of waiting. But with dedication, a commitment to learning, and patience, achieving your goals is within reach. By adhering to the guidance in this book and maintaining determination, there's a strong possibility that you'll not only achieve monetization but also establish a distinct presence on YouTube.

Wishing you every success in your endeavors.

Best regards,

Jake Radford.

Disclaimer

All advice provided in this book is based on experience and extensive research. It's important to recognize that algorithms, statistics, and online services are constantly evolving in our dynamic digital world. While this book aims to offer insights that transcend mere data, its primary goal is to instil confidence and offer a fresh perspective on YouTube creation. Efforts have been made to provide contemporary advice, including the utilization of Artificial Intelligence. However, at the heart of all content creation, the most crucial element remains the satisfaction of the viewer. Platforms like Google and YouTube will always prioritize this. It is essential for readers to stay updated with the latest trends and consult professionals when necessary. The author and publisher are not responsible for any actions taken based on the content of this book. Always seek expert guidance tailored to your unique situation. All comments and suggestions related to monetization within this book are provided as advice and general information. It is essential for readers to conduct their own thorough research and consult with a trained accountant or financial advisor regarding tax implications and other financial matters specific to their individual circumstances. The author and publisher are not responsible for any financial decisions or actions taken based on the content of this book. Always seek professional guidance when it comes to your unique financial situation. Some links provided within this book may be affiliate links, and if you make a purchase through these links, we may receive a commission at no additional cost to you.

Contents

Preface 2

Disclaimer 4

Chapter 1: Youtube Introduction and Niche Selection 6

Chapter 2: Setting Up Your New YouTube Channel 13

Chapter 3: Preparing Your First Video 21

Chapter 4: Titles, Thumbnails, and Descriptions 33

Chapter 5: Monetization Basics 41

Chapter 6: Advanced Monetization Strategies 47

Chapter 7: YouTube Shorts and Reels 55

Chapter 8: Faceless Channels 59

Chapter 9: AI Power: Advanced Faceless Channel Strategies 63

Chapter 10: Social Media and Marketing Strategies 70

Chapter 11: Analytics and Performance Metrics 76

Chapter 12: Delayed Gratification 81

Chapter 1: Youtube Introduction and Niche Selection

In the digital age, few platforms have revolutionized the way we consume content as profoundly as YouTube. Born on Valentine's Day in 2005, this video-sharing platform was the brainchild of three innovative minds: Steve Chen, Chad Hurley, and Jawed Karim. Little did they know that their creation would become a cornerstone of modern digital culture. Fast forward to today, and YouTube is no longer just a website; it's a cultural phenomenon. Owned by Google, it stands as the second most frequented online destination, surpassed only by Google's own search engine.

The numbers speak volumes about YouTube's staggering reach. With a user base exceeding 2.5 billion people each month, the platform is more than just a collection of videos: it's a global community. And what keeps this community thriving? Content, and lots of it. Every single day, users collectively consume over one billion hours of video, ranging from educational tutorials to entertainment and everything in between.

But what makes YouTube truly exceptional isn't just its impressive statistics; it's the transformative impact it has had on content creation and consumption. Gone are the days when television and print media held a monopoly over public attention. YouTube has democratized the field, allowing anyone with a camera and an internet connection to reach a global audience. It's a platform where creativity knows no bounds, and where niche interests can find not just a spotlight, but a stage of their own.

As we delve deeper into the starting, growing, and monetizing of a YouTube channel, it's crucial to understand this historical context. The platform's evolution from a simple video-sharing site to a multifaceted ecosystem offers invaluable lessons for aspiring YouTubers. It's a testament to the limitless possibilities that await those willing to invest time, effort, and creativity into their channel.

Understanding YouTube's past is the first step in shaping your future on the platform. The journey ahead is filled with opportunities, challenges, and the potential for unprecedented success.

"Why YouTube?" The answer is as multifaceted as the platform itself. YouTube has democratized content creation in a way that no other platform has. With its user-friendly interface and robust community, it has become the go-to destination for anyone looking to share their voice, their vision, or their expertise. The platform is a treasure trove of content, offering everything from beauty tutorials and product reviews to gaming channels and unboxing videos. The diversity is not just in the types of content but also in the people who create it.

Take, for example, the meteoric rise of Mr. Beast, a name that has become synonymous with viral content and philanthropy. With a subscriber count exceeding 1.8 million at the time of writing this book, Mr. Beast's journey is a testament to the transformative power of hard work and dedication. He began his YouTube career at the tender age of 13, initially focusing on video game walkthroughs. Over the years, his content evolved, blending philanthropy with grand and often outrageous challenges and stunts. His story is a vivid illustration of how YouTube can serve as a launchpad for anyone with a vision.

The platform's accessibility and broad content spectrum mean that there's something for everyone, both in terms of creation and consumption. Whether you're an aspiring makeup artist, a tech enthusiast, or someone with a unique skill set, YouTube offers you a platform to share your talents with the world. And for viewers, the options are virtually limitless. Whether you want to learn a new skill, catch up on current events, or simply be entertained, YouTube has you covered.

But beyond the content and the creators, what sets YouTube apart is its community. The interaction between creators and their audience is unparalleled. Comments, likes, and shares don't just serve as metrics; they are a form of dialogue, a way for creators to engage with their viewers and for viewers to have a say in the content they consume. This symbiotic relationship fosters a sense of belonging, making both creators and viewers feel like part of something bigger than themselves.

Remember that you're joining a vibrant, global community. It's a place where creativity is celebrated, where hard work is rewarded, and where anyone with a story to tell or a skill to share can find an audience. And who knows? With the right mix of dedication, talent, and a little bit of luck, you might just become the next Mr. Beast, or better yet, a unique success story all your own.

Continuing from the compelling reasons to choose YouTube as your platform, let's delve into what is often referred to as the YouTube ecosystem. Now, don't let the term "ecosystem" intimidate you. Think of it as a bustling city where everyone has a role to play. In this city, you're not just a resident; you're also a contributor. You have the power to shape its culture, its content, and its conversations.

The YouTube ecosystem is made up of several key components, each serving a unique purpose. First and foremost are the creators—that's you! You're the heartbeat of this ecosystem, bringing life to it with your content. Whether you're sharing cooking recipes, travel vlogs, or educational tutorials, you're adding value to the platform.

Next, we have the viewers, the people who tune in to watch your videos. They're your audience, your fans, and your critics. They're the ones who will like your videos, share them, and comment on them. Their engagement is not just a morale booster; it's also a crucial factor that YouTube's algorithm considers when deciding how widely to distribute your content.

Then there's the algorithm itself, the behind-the-scenes maestro that determines which videos get seen by whom. While the algorithm may seem like a mystery, understanding its basic principles can significantly boost your channel's growth. It's designed to keep viewers on the platform for as long as possible by showing them content that they're likely to enjoy. That's why understanding your audience and creating content that resonates with them is so important.

Another key player in this ecosystem is advertising. Once you meet certain criteria, YouTube allows you to monetize your channel through ads. These ads are what make it possible for many creators to turn their passion into a full-time job. But it's not just about making money; it's also about partnerships and sponsorships that can come your way once you've built a sizable audience.

Last but not least, there's the community aspect. YouTube isn't just a platform for sharing videos; it's also a social network where you can interact with viewers and other creators. This interaction can take many forms, from responding to comments on your videos to collaborating with other creators. It's this sense of community that turns a collection of videos into a dynamic, interactive experience.

So, as you prepare to join this vibrant ecosystem, remember that you're not just a passive participant. You're an active contributor with the power to shape your own destiny and, in the process, enrich the platform for everyone involved. As we move on to the technical aspects of setting up your channel, keep in mind that you're laying the foundation for your place in this exciting, ever-evolving ecosystem.

Continuing from the understanding of YouTube's dynamic ecosystem, let's address a pivotal decision every aspiring YouTuber faces: choosing a niche. The term "niche" might sound like industry jargon, but it's really just a focused area of interest. Think of it as your specialty, the subject matter you'll become known for. Selecting the right niche isn't just a preliminary step; it's a strategic move that can set the tone for your entire YouTube journey.

Now, there are two main approaches to selecting a niche.

The first approach to selecting a niche is to let your passion be your guide. When you're genuinely invested in the subject matter of your content, it shines through in ways that are both subtle and impactful. Viewers are incredibly perceptive; they can easily distinguish between creators who are going through the motions and those who are truly passionate about what they're sharing. This authenticity becomes a magnet for engagement, drawing viewers into not just the topic at hand, but also into your unique perspective and enthusiasm for it. Whether your passion lies in cooking sumptuous meals, exploring far-off places, dissecting the latest tech gadgets, or any other subject, that love for what you do becomes infectious. Your excitement seeps through the screen, captivating your audience and making them eager for more. Moreover, when you're passionate about your niche, the often arduous process of content creation becomes a labor of love. You'll find yourself looking forward to filming the next video, researching new topics, and even diving into the editing process. In short, following your passion doesn't just make for better content; it also enhances your own experience as a creator, making each step of your YouTube journey not just a means to an end, but a rewarding endeavor in its own right.

The second approach is a bit more analytical and is ideal for those who are entering the YouTube space primarily as a business venture. In this case, you'll want to do some market research to identify trending topics. There are several online tools to help you gauge what's hot and what's not. For instance, Google Trends can provide valuable insights into what people are currently searching for. The Explore Page on YouTube is another great resource, offering a snapshot of trending videos and topics. For those who want to dive even deeper, vidIQ offers a range of analytics and educational resources to help you understand what works and what doesn't on YouTube. They even have a handy Google Chrome extension that allows you to analyze YouTube data right from your browser.

If you're considering tools to help you navigate the YouTube landscape, it's worth noting that vidIQ offers more advanced features through its paid plans. While the basic version provides some useful insights, the paid plans offer a more comprehensive analysis that could be invaluable for channel growth. And here's a bit of good news: at the time of writing this book, you can get a healthy discount on vidIQ's paid plans by using the following link: **www.vidiq.com/promo25**. It's an investment that could pay off significantly as you work to optimize your channel and reach a wider audience.

Whether you're following your heart or the data, the key is to choose a niche that you can commit to. Consistency is crucial in the YouTube world, and it's much easier to be consistent when you're either passionate about your niche or confident in its market potential.

So, as you lay the groundwork for your YouTube channel, take some time to think about your niche. It's a decision that will influence everything from the content you create to the audience you attract. And remember, the right niche isn't just about what's popular; it's about what you can sustain and grow over the long term. As we transition into the practical steps of setting up your channel, keep your chosen niche in mind. It will serve as your guiding light, illuminating the path ahead and making your YouTube journey not just successful, but also deeply rewarding.

Chapter 2: Setting Up Your New YouTube Channel

In this chapter, we'll navigate the initial waters of creating a Google account, a gateway to the YouTube world. From there, the focus shifts to the visual elements, the first impressions: setting up a profile photo that captures the essence of the creator or the channel's theme, and designing a banner that stands as a testament to the channel's ethos. But visuals, while crucial, are just one piece of the puzzle. Crafting a compelling channel description is akin to laying down a welcome mat, inviting viewers to explore further, to stay, to engage. And finally, to ensure a seamless experience for both creators and viewers, we'll delve into the significance and process of verifying the account.

The first order of business is creating a Google Account. Think of this account as your passport to the digital world of YouTube. It's not just an email and a password; it's the gateway to your online presence, and it's easier to set up than you might think.

If you're planning to use YouTube for business purposes, there's an option to turn on business personalization when you create your Google Account. This feature not only enhances your experience but also paves the way for setting up a Google Business Profile. This profile can be a game-changer in terms of increasing your business visibility online and managing your digital footprint effectively.

Creating a Google Account is straightforward, but it's crucial to provide accurate personal information. This isn't just about filling in blanks on a form; it's about security. The more accurate your information, the more secure your account will be, and the more personalized your experience across Google services.

Now, let's get into the nitty-gritty of setting up your account. Contrary to popular belief, you don't need a Gmail address to create a Google Account. If you have an existing non-Gmail email, you can use that instead. To start, navigate to the Google Account sign-in page and click on 'Create account.' You'll be prompted to enter your name and choose a username. Then, you'll need to create and confirm a password. A quick tip for mobile users: the first letter of your password won't be case-sensitive. After this, you'll click 'Next.'

At this point, you'll have the option to add and verify a phone number for your account. While this step is optional, it's highly recommended for added security. Once you've entered your phone number and clicked 'Next,' you're almost there.

If you prefer to use an existing email address, the process is just as simple. On the Google Account sign-in page, click 'Create account' and then select the option that says 'Use my current email address instead.' Enter your existing email, click 'Next,' and you'll receive a verification code. Once you enter this code and click 'Verify,' your Google Account will be up and running.

Congratulations, you've just taken the first step in your YouTube journey! With your Google Account in place, you're now ready to dive into the exciting world of channel creation, content planning, and audience engagement. But before we get ahead of ourselves, let's focus on the next crucial step: setting up your YouTube channel.

To initiate your YouTube journey, start by signing into YouTube. This can be done on a computer or through the mobile site using the same credentials as your Google Account. Once logged in, navigate to the profile section, usually represented by your profile picture. Here, you'll find an option to 'Create a channel'. By clicking on this, you'll be prompted to confirm the creation of your channel. The platform will automatically use the name and photo associated with your Google Account, but don't worry, these can be customized later to better reflect your channel's identity.

For those who have a vision of a more specialized channel, perhaps representing a business, a community group, or any other entity, YouTube offers the flexibility to name your channel differently from your personal Google name. After selecting the 'Create a channel' option, you'll be presented with a choice to use a different name. This is particularly useful if you're aiming to build a distinct brand identity on the platform.

Once you've decided on the name and filled in the necessary details, a simple click on 'Create' will bring your channel to life. As your channel grows and evolves, you might consider adding other members to help manage it. YouTube provides options to add managers, ensuring that the channel can be a collaborative effort if desired.

With your channel now set up, you're ready to dive into the world of content creation, audience engagement, and all the other exciting opportunities YouTube has to offer.

Countless YouTube channels vie for attention, your profile photo stands as a beacon, offering viewers a glimpse into the essence of your channel. This seemingly modest image carries the weight of first impressions, making its selection and design crucial.

For those who might not be naturally inclined towards design, platforms like Canva can be a lifesaver. Canva's intuitive interface allows even novices to craft striking logos or designs that mirror their channel's ethos. With a rich array of templates and design tools, creating a visual representation of your brand becomes a breeze.

Yet, while logos have their charm, there's an undeniable appeal to using a personal photograph. Many YouTubers lean into this approach, and for good reason. A well-chosen personal photo, particularly one where the creator engages directly with the camera, can establish an immediate rapport with viewers. It's a nod to authenticity, signaling that behind the videos and the content is a real individual with genuine experiences and stories to share. This personal touch can be a magnet for credibility, drawing viewers into a more intimate and trusting relationship with the creator.

The decision between a logo and a personal photo hinges on the image and connection you aim to foster with your audience. If your channel leans towards a more formal or business-oriented vibe, a polished logo might be more apt. Conversely, if your content is deeply intertwined with your personal journey and experiences, a photo could be the ideal choice.

Once you've settled on the perfect image, it's time to upload it to YouTube. To do this, sign in to your YouTube account and click on your current profile picture, usually found at the top right corner. From the dropdown menu, select 'Your Channel' and then click on 'Customize Channel'. Here, you'll find the option to change your profile photo. Simply click on the camera icon, select your chosen image from your device, and save. Voilà! Your YouTube channel now proudly displays your chosen profile photo, ready to greet every visitor.

Your channel banner acts as a headline, setting the stage for what viewers can expect. This expansive image, stretching across the top of your channel, offers a canvas to communicate your brand's message, style, and ethos. Given its prominence, investing time and thought into its design is paramount.

For those not well-versed in graphic design, online tools like Canva can be invaluable. Canva's user-friendly platform provides a multitude of templates specifically tailored for YouTube banners, ensuring the dimensions are just right. With drag-and-drop features, a rich library of images, and customizable text options, even beginners can craft banners that look professional and engaging.

However, if you're seeking a truly unique design or don't trust your own design instincts, turning to professionals can be a wise choice. Platforms like Fiverr offer a marketplace teeming with talented graphic designers. The beauty of Fiverr lies in its range; whether you're on a tight budget or willing to invest a bit more for premium design, there's likely a freelancer who fits the bill. By collaborating with a designer, you can bring your vision to life, ensuring your banner not only looks great but also aligns perfectly with your channel's identity.

Once your banner is ready, showcasing it on YouTube is a straightforward process. Begin by logging into your YouTube account. Navigate to your channel page and hover over the banner area. You'll notice a camera or pencil icon appearing at the top right corner of the banner. Clicking on this will allow you to upload your new banner. Ensure the image aligns well within the provided frame, make any necessary adjustments, and then save. Your channel will now proudly display your new banner, offering viewers a visually appealing introduction to your content.

Remember, your banner is more than just a decorative element. It's a powerful communication tool, conveying at a glance what your channel is all about. Whether you opt for a DIY approach or seek professional assistance, ensure your banner resonates with your brand's voice and the content you produce. As your channel evolves, don't hesitate to revisit and refresh your banner, ensuring it remains relevant and engaging.

A channel description isn't just a formality; it's an opportunity. It's your chance to succinctly communicate the essence of your content, the value you offer, and the journey you're inviting viewers to embark on. Central to this is the idea of a niche or a core theme. By honing in on a specific subject or area of expertise, you provide clarity. Viewers, when they stumble upon your channel, should immediately grasp what your content is about and, more importantly, what they stand to gain from it.

Imagine a viewer, curious and eager to learn, browsing through YouTube. When they come across your channel, the description should speak directly to their interests or needs. It should answer the question: "Why should I watch these videos?" By articulating what viewers will learn or experience, you give them a compelling reason to click, watch, and eventually, hit that subscribe button.

But crafting such a description requires thought and precision. Start by identifying your channel's unique selling point. What sets you apart? Is it your unique approach to a popular topic? Or perhaps it's your expertise in a niche area? Once you've pinpointed this, weave it into a concise narrative. Remember, brevity is key. In a few sentences, encapsulate the essence of your channel, ensuring it's both informative and inviting.

A channel description is more than just a few lines on a page. It's a strategic tool, a beacon that guides potential subscribers to your content. By clearly defining your niche and articulating the value you offer, you set the stage for growth, engagement, and a thriving community of loyal viewers. As we continue our journey into the world of YouTube, remember that every element, from banners to descriptions, plays a role in crafting your channel's unique story.

YouTube requires a few essential steps, and one of the pivotal moments in this journey is verifying your account. This isn't just a formality; it's a gateway to unlocking a broader range of features and ensuring a smoother experience for both you and your audience.

So, why is verification important? At its core, it's about trust and authenticity. YouTube wants to ensure that real individuals or entities are behind the channels, and this process helps in maintaining the platform's credibility. By verifying, you're not only confirming your identity but also assuring YouTube and your potential audience of your genuine intent.

The process is straightforward. When you initiate the verification, YouTube will prompt you to provide a phone number. Don't fret; this isn't about intruding into your privacy. It's a simple mechanism to send you a verification code, either through a text message or a voice call. Once you receive this code, inputting it back into YouTube completes the verification.

Now, what's the reward for this small effort? A significant one! After verifying, you're no longer restricted to the standard 15-minute limit for your videos. Imagine the possibilities! Lengthier tutorials, extended vlogs, or comprehensive reviews – the platform is now your oyster.

Additionally, there might be times when Google, YouTube's parent company, requires further confirmation of your identity. This could be to ensure you meet age requirements for specific content or to access certain features. In such instances, a valid ID might be requested. This step is to ensure that the platform remains safe, credible, and adheres to its guidelines.

Moreover, post-I.D verification, creators gain the ability to add external links in their videos using the 'i' icon, enhancing the interactive experience for viewers and directing them to additional resources or affiliated sites. Links can also be added to the description page on your main channel.

In essence, verification is like getting a badge of authenticity. It's a small step, but one that paves the way for a richer YouTube experience. As you journey further into content creation, remember that trust and authenticity are invaluable currencies. Verification is just the beginning of building that rapport with your audience and the platform.

Chapter 3: Preparing Your First Video

It's not just about creating content; it's about crafting content with purpose, direction, and a clear vision. Chapter 3 dives deep into the art of planning your content, ensuring that every video you produce aligns with your goals and resonates with your target audience.

Starting with the basics, it's essential to define the goals for your YouTube channel. Are you aiming to educate, entertain, inspire, or perhaps a mix of all three? By setting clear objectives, you provide your channel with a roadmap, guiding your content decisions and giving your work a sense of purpose.

Once you've set your goals, it's time to turn your attention to your audience. Who are they? What are their interests, needs, and preferences? By researching and understanding your target demographic, you can tailor your content to meet their expectations, ensuring higher engagement and loyalty.

But understanding your audience is just one piece of the puzzle. It's equally crucial to be aware of your competitors. What are they doing right? Where can you differentiate and offer unique value? By researching competitors, you gain insights that can shape your content strategy, ensuring you stand out in the crowded YouTube landscape.

With a clear understanding of your goals, audience, and competition, you're now equipped to plan your content. This is where creativity meets strategy. Think about the topics that will resonate most with your audience, the kind of videos they're eager to watch, and how you can deliver that content in an engaging manner.

Execution is the next step. With a plan in hand, it's time to bring your vision to life. This involves everything from choosing the right topic to setting up your recording environment. For those just starting, understanding the basics of YouTube equipment is crucial. You don't need the most expensive gear, but knowing what's essential for beginners can set you on the right path. Whether you're recording your desktop for tutorials or filming in a studio setup, ensuring good video and audio quality is paramount.

Once your content is recorded, the magic of editing begins. This process allows you to refine your video, ensuring it's polished, engaging, and ready for your audience.

But don't stop at YouTube. Your videos have the potential to shine across various social networks. Repurposing your content for different platforms can expand your reach and introduce your channel to a broader audience.

Always be in the mode of evaluation. After publishing, monitor the performance of your videos. Are they meeting your goals? Are they resonating with your audience? Based on these insights, adjust your strategy as needed, ensuring continuous growth and engagement.

Evaluation is not just a one-time task; it's an ongoing commitment to excellence. After publishing your videos, it's essential to dive deep into YouTube's built-in analytics tool. This powerful feature provides a wealth of data that can offer invaluable insights into your video's performance.

Begin by examining the basic metrics: views, likes, dislikes, and comments. These will give you a preliminary understanding of how well your content is being received. However, to truly gauge the effectiveness of your videos, you need to delve deeper.

Watch time, for instance, is a critical metric. It indicates the total number of minutes that viewers have spent watching your videos on YouTube. A higher watch time suggests that viewers are finding your content engaging and are spending more time on your channel. If you notice a decline or stagnation in watch time, it might be an indicator to reevaluate the content's pacing, length, or subject matter.

Audience retention is another vital metric. It shows you the percentage of your video that viewers are watching. If you notice a significant drop at a specific point in your video, it might indicate that a particular segment was not engaging or perhaps confusing. This feedback can guide you in making future content more captivating.

Demographics provide insights into the age, gender, and geographical location of your viewers. This data can help you tailor your content to better suit the preferences and interests of your primary audience.

Engagement metrics, such as likes, shares, and comments, can offer a qualitative measure of how your content is resonating with viewers. A video with a high number of shares, for instance, indicates that viewers found it compelling enough to share with their network.

Lastly, the traffic source metric can show you where your views are coming from, be it direct searches, suggested videos, or external sources. This can help you understand which promotional strategies are working and where there might be opportunities to expand your reach.

In essence, YouTube's analytics is a goldmine of information. By regularly reviewing and interpreting this data, you can make informed decisions about your content strategy. Adjustments based on analytics are not about second-guessing your creativity but about refining it, ensuring that your content remains aligned with your goals and continues to resonate with your ever-evolving audience.

Before diving into content creation, it's essential to equip oneself with the right tools. While the charm of a video often lies in its content, the quality can significantly influence viewer retention and overall channel growth. Thankfully, in today's digital age, achieving professional-grade video quality doesn't necessarily require a Hollywood budget.

For those who prefer staying behind the scenes, there's an entire chapter later on (Chapter 9) dedicated to creating compelling faceless YouTube channels. But for now, let's focus on those who wish to be in front of the camera.

First and foremost, a good camera is indispensable. However, if investing in a high-end camera isn't feasible right away, many modern smartphones come equipped with cameras that can capture high-definition videos. With the right techniques, a smartphone can rival the output of many dedicated cameras.

Sound quality is just as crucial as video quality. While many cameras and phones have built-in microphones, for clearer and more professional-sounding audio, an external microphone is a worthy investment. Whether it's a clip-on lapel mic or a standalone one, good audio can make a world of difference in viewer experience.

Stability is key. No one enjoys a shaky video. A tripod can help in achieving steady shots, making videos look more polished and professional. There are various tripods available, from tabletop versions to full-sized ones, ensuring there's something for every kind of content creator.

Lighting can transform a video. Even the best cameras can't compensate for poor lighting. A basic lighting kit, which might include softboxes or ring lights, can illuminate the subject evenly, reducing shadows and enhancing video quality.

Of course, equipment isn't just about the tangible items. One's creativity, ideas, and passion—what we'll refer to as 'creative mental assets'—are just as vital. These are the unique perspectives and spins that a creator brings to their content, setting them apart from others.

Lastly, once the recording is done, the magic of editing begins. Editing software helps in refining the video, cutting out mistakes, adding effects, and making the content more engaging. For beginners, iMovie offers a user-friendly interface. As one becomes more proficient, they might consider transitioning to more advanced software like Final Cut Pro or Adobe Premiere Pro CC.

In summary, while having the right equipment can enhance video quality, it's the passion, dedication, and unique perspective of the creator that truly makes a YouTube channel shine. Equip yourself both tangibly and mentally, and the path to YouTube success becomes clearer and more achievable. While the technical aspects of recording are undeniably important, the heart of any successful video lies in the presenter's authenticity. The way one presents, their confidence, and their genuine attitude play pivotal roles in making content not just watchable, but truly likable.

Being genuine on camera is an art in itself. It's about letting one's true self shine through, without the layers of pretense or the pressure of perfection. When viewers sense authenticity, they connect more deeply with the content. They're not just watching a video; they're engaging with a real person, with real emotions, experiences, and stories.

However, it's natural to feel a bit uneasy or self-conscious when starting out. The lens of a camera can initially feel like a judgmental eye, analyzing every move and every word. But here's a comforting thought: just like any new endeavor, the initial discomfort is temporary. Remember the first time you tried riding a bike or learning a new language? It wasn't second nature from the get-go. It took practice, patience, and perseverance. The same principle applies to recording videos. With each recording, the process becomes more familiar, the nerves settle, and confidence grows.

As you produce more videos, you'll notice a shift. The camera will start to feel less like a critic and more like a friend, a confidant to whom you're sharing your thoughts and ideas. This transition doesn't happen overnight, but with persistence, it's inevitable.

Moreover, it's essential to remember that every seasoned YouTuber, every familiar face that seems so at ease in front of the camera, started somewhere. They too had their initial moments of doubt, their first videos that perhaps they look back on with a mix of nostalgia and cringe. But they kept going, learned from their experiences, and honed their craft.

While mastering the technicalities of recording is crucial, the soul of your content lies in your authenticity. Embrace the journey, be patient with yourself, and remember that with each video, you're not just creating content; you're growing, evolving, and inching closer to the best version of your YouTube self.

For those new to videography, the realm of camera effects and movements might seem a tad overwhelming. Terms like 'panning', 'tilting', 'tracking', and 'zooming' might sound like a foreign language. But fear not, because the digital age has made learning these techniques more accessible than ever.

The internet is a treasure trove of information. A simple search on Google can open doors to countless tutorials, articles, and video demonstrations that break down these techniques. From understanding the basics of framing to mastering the art of the smooth dolly shot, there's a guide for everything. Websites, forums, and online courses offer in-depth insights, often accompanied by visual examples, making the learning process interactive and engaging.

But, as with any skill, merely reading or watching isn't enough. The real learning happens when you pick up your camera and start experimenting. Try out different shots, play with angles, and see how varying movements can change the mood and feel of a scene. It's through this hands-on approach that the theoretical knowledge transforms into practical expertise.

Moreover, the YouTube community itself is a valuable resource. Many seasoned YouTubers share their experiences, tips, and tricks, offering insights into their journey of mastering the craft. By studying their content, not just as a viewer but as a budding creator, you can glean valuable lessons. Pay attention to how they frame their shots, how they use lighting, or how they employ movement to tell a story.

Remember, every great videographer started as a beginner. They too had their moments of trial and error, their initial videos where things didn't go as planned. But with persistence, a thirst for knowledge, and the willingness to learn from mistakes, they honed their skills.

The journey to mastering camera techniques is a blend of research, practice, and continuous learning. Embrace the process, be curious, and let every recording be an opportunity to learn and improve. With dedication and passion, you'll not only understand the intricacies of your camera but also the art of storytelling through your lens.

First impressions matter immensely. The initial few seconds of your video, the intro, can be the deciding factor for a viewer to continue watching or move on. Similarly, the outro, the concluding segment, plays a pivotal role in guiding your audience towards further engagement. Crafting compelling intros and outros can significantly enhance the viewer experience and boost your channel's identity.

Start by pinpointing your unique style. Are you quirky and fun, or more on the serious and informative side? Your style will dictate the tone and feel of your intro and outro. Once you've identified this, consider incorporating animations. A lively animation can instantly grab attention, setting the stage for the content that follows. But remember, while animations can be captivating, they should align with your overall brand and message.

Audio is another crucial element. The right background music can set the mood, whether it's upbeat, dramatic, or calming. However, ensure that the audio complements the visuals and doesn't overshadow your content.

Now, while your intro draws viewers in, your outro should guide them towards a specific action. This is where a Call to Action (CTA) comes in. Whether you're asking viewers to like, share, subscribe, or check out another video, make your CTA clear and compelling.

In the realm of intros and outros, less is often more. Aim for brevity. A concise, impactful intro or outro can be more effective than a lengthy one that risks losing viewer interest. Think of it as a brief handshake or a quick wave, a momentary interaction that leaves a lasting impression.

Branding is paramount. Whether it's through a logo, specific color schemes, or unique graphics, ensure that your intros and outros resonate with your brand's identity. This consistency not only reinforces brand recall but also builds trust with your audience.

Eye-catching visuals are a must. Whether it's through vibrant illustrations, dynamic animations, or a simple title card, your intro and outro should be visually appealing. Typography, the art of arranging text in a visually pleasing manner, can also play a significant role. Choose fonts and text layouts that align with your brand and are easy to read.

Intros and outros are more than just bookends to your content; they're powerful tools that can amplify your brand's voice, engage viewers, and drive action. By focusing on clarity, branding, and visual appeal, and by keeping things short and sweet, you can craft intros and outros that not only enhance your videos but also leave a lasting mark on your audience.

Your first Youtube video upload is a momentous occasion. It's the beginning of a journey where you share your voice, passion, and creativity with a global audience. But, as with any journey, it's essential to start on the right foot.

First and foremost, the power of keywords cannot be overstated. When you're preparing to upload, think about the terms your potential viewers might use to search for content like yours. Incorporate these keywords naturally into your video title, description, and tags. This simple step can significantly enhance your video's visibility, making it easier for viewers to discover your content.

VIDIQ is a powerful tool that has become indispensable for many YouTubers, especially when it comes to keyword research. This platform offers a comprehensive suite of features that delve deep into the intricacies of YouTube's algorithm, helping creators understand which keywords are trending, how they rank, and how they can be best utilized for maximum visibility. By suggesting relevant keywords based on your content and showing their search volume, competition, and overall score, VIDIQ simplifies the often daunting task of SEO

optimization. With its insights, creators can craft titles, descriptions, and tags that significantly enhance discoverability, ensuring that their content reaches its intended audience and stands out in a crowded digital landscape. You can get a healthy discount on vidIQ's paid plans by using the following link:
www.vidiq.com/promo25

Now, while your video might be a visual masterpiece, don't forget about the auditory aspect. Adding closed captions can make your content accessible to a broader audience, including those who might be hearing impaired or those who prefer to watch videos without sound. Moreover, captions can also boost your video's searchability, as they provide additional text that search engines can index.

As you venture further into content creation, always have your target audience in mind. Who are you creating for? What are their interests, preferences, and behaviors? By understanding your audience, you can tailor your content to resonate more deeply with them, ensuring higher engagement and loyalty.

Consistency is key in the world of YouTube. Once you've decided on a publishing schedule, whether it's once a week, bi-weekly, or even daily, stick to it. Regular uploads can help you build a dedicated viewer base eagerly awaiting your next piece of content.

But, what truly sets a video apart is the value it offers. Whether it's entertainment, education, or inspiration, ensure that every video you upload brings something unique to the table. This genuine value is what will keep viewers coming back for more.

And once your video is live, don't just rely on YouTube's platform for visibility. Cross-promote your content on other social media platforms, blogs, or websites. This multi-channel approach can help you reach a wider audience and drive more traffic to your YouTube channel.

Now, for the practical bit: uploading your video. Begin by signing into your YouTube account. Click on the camera icon at the top right, then select 'Upload Video.' From here, you can drag and drop your video file or select it from your device. While your video uploads, fill in the title, description, and tags, ensuring you incorporate those crucial keywords. Once uploaded, review your video settings, add any end screens or cards if desired, and when you're satisfied, hit 'Publish.'

One of the primary concerns when incorporating music into videos is the potential for copyright issues. If you're not careful about the music you choose, you might find yourself facing monetization challenges or even legal disputes. This is because the rights to most songs belong to copyright holders, and they have the authority to decide how their music is used on platforms like YouTube. If you use a copyrighted song without proper permissions, your video might receive a Content ID claim, indicating that you've used copyrighted content. Such claims can affect the availability of your video and might even lead to monetization restrictions.

So, how can creators avoid these pitfalls? While some video editing software might offer a selection of sounds and songs as part of their package, it's essential to ensure that these tracks are truly royalty-free and cleared for use on YouTube. One of the safest and most straightforward solutions is to utilize the YouTube Audio Library. This library is a treasure trove of high-quality, royalty-free music and sound effects. Each track is available at a crisp 320kbps, ensuring that your videos have the best audio quality. The best part? These tracks are free for YouTube creators and can be directly downloaded and integrated into your videos.

By using the YouTube Audio Library, creators can sidestep the complexities of music licensing. Not only does this ensure that your videos remain free from copyright claims, but it also provides peace of mind, knowing that the music enhancing your content won't lead to unforeseen issues down the line. In essence, while music is a powerful tool for content creators, it's crucial to approach its use with caution and knowledge, ensuring that your creative endeavors remain both harmonious and hassle-free.

Chapter 4: Titles, Thumbnails, and Descriptions

Mr. Beast, a titan in the YouTube community, has often emphasized the paramount importance of thumbnails and concise descriptions in capturing a viewer's attention. It's these visual and succinct cues that act as the hook, reeling in potential viewers. But while these elements grab attention, the description plays a subtler, yet equally crucial role. It provides depth and context, feeding the algorithm the necessary information to appropriately position and present the video to potential viewers. This information, combined with the speech and content of the video, is processed by the algorithm to determine the most appropriate audience for the video.

A compelling YouTube title is the shining lighthouse guiding viewers to your video. It's the first impression, the initial hook, and often the deciding factor for a potential viewer. Crafting the perfect title is an art, and understanding its nuances can significantly boost your video's visibility and engagement.

First and foremost, ensure that your title genuinely reflects the content of your video. Misleading titles might get clicks initially, but they'll also lead to quick drop-offs and potentially negative feedback. Remember, trust is paramount, and you want to build a loyal audience base that knows they can rely on your content.

Understanding your audience is crucial. Who are they? What are they searching for? What problems are they trying to solve? By knowing your target demographic, you can tailor your titles to speak directly to them. This is where keyword research comes into play. Tools like VIDIQ can be invaluable in identifying trending keywords that resonate with your audience.

A little formatting trick that's been proven effective is the use of brackets in your title. They can provide additional context or highlight a unique aspect of your video. Similarly, instilling a sense of urgency or curiosity can prompt viewers to click on your video amidst a sea of alternatives. Starting your title with words like "how," "why," and "when" can pique curiosity and improve click-through rates.

Brevity is your friend. Short and punchy titles are more likely to capture attention. Moreover, adding the current year to your title can make your content seem timely and relevant. Let's look at some examples to illustrate the difference:

Negative Vague Title:
"Make money online with these methods as it will help you get really rich!"

Positive Conise, Short and Direct Title:
"10 Secret Ways I Made Money Online In (2023)"

Negative Long-winded Low Interest Title:
"Psychopaths are bad and can do horrible things to you which can make your life a misery"

Positive Effective Longer Title:
"Detect When a PSYCHOPATH is Trying to Control You (2023) "

In essence, your title should be a clear, concise, and compelling invitation to your content. It's the gateway to your video, and with the right approach, it can significantly amplify your reach and engagement. The thumbnail you select must match and compliment the title with its text and image story.

In the bustling digital streets of YouTube, your video thumbnail is akin to a billboard. It's the visual cue that can either draw viewers in or have them scroll past. Given its significance, crafting an effective thumbnail isn't just about aesthetics; it's a strategic move that can significantly impact your video's success.

Firstly, ensure you're using the right dimensions for your thumbnail. A distorted or pixelated image can deter potential viewers. Once you've got the size right, the background image you choose is paramount. Opt for a high-quality, captivating photo that's relevant to your video's content. This image is the canvas upon which you'll layer other elements.

Text is a vital component of a thumbnail. It provides context and can amplify the message of your video. However, don't just slap on any text. It should be concise, legible, and complementary to your video title. The font style you choose can also play a role in conveying the mood or theme of your video. Bright backgrounds can enhance the contrast, making the text pop, and if there's one color that's been observed to grab attention, it's yellow. Incorporating yellow, where appropriate, can give your thumbnail an edge.

Branding isn't just for corporations. As a content creator, you too have a brand, a unique identity that sets you apart. Consistency in your thumbnails, whether it's a particular color scheme, font, or logo, can make your videos instantly recognizable to your audience. This familiarity can lead to higher click-through rates.

Faces, especially those making direct eye contact, have been shown to be particularly engaging. It creates a connection, a momentary bond between the creator and the potential viewer. If relevant, include a face in your thumbnail. It humanizes your content and can evoke emotions even before the video is played.

While designing, always remember that many viewers will be on mobile devices. Ensure your thumbnail is legible and impactful even on smaller screens. And don't operate in a vacuum. Take a look at what your competitors are doing. Not to copy, but to understand the trends and perhaps identify gaps that you can fill. In the quest for crafting the perfect thumbnail, one cannot underestimate the power of research. By analyzing successful YouTube videos with high view counts, you can glean insights into what truly resonates with viewers. These popular videos serve as real-time case studies, showcasing trends, styles, and elements that have already proven to be effective in capturing attention. Observing patterns, such as color combinations, text placements, or the kind of imagery used, can offer invaluable guidance. It's not about mimicking what's already out there, but rather understanding the underlying principles of what works and then infusing those learnings with your unique touch. Remember, the goal is to stand out, but with a foundation rooted in proven success.

Lastly, while there are numerous tools available for thumbnail creation, Adobe Photoshop and Canva Pro stand out. Photoshop, with its extensive features, is a favorite among many YouTubers. It offers flexibility and precision, allowing even those with minimal design experience to craft compelling thumbnails. Canva Pro, with its user-friendly interface and vast template library, is another excellent option.

Thumbnails are more than just an image. It's a promise of the value your video offers. It's the first impression, and as the saying goes, you only get one chance to make a first impression. Make it count.

The description beneath each video plays a pivotal role. As touched upon earlier, descriptions aren't just a mere afterthought; they're a strategic tool. They serve as a bridge, guiding viewers to additional resources, be it your personal website or affiliate links that resonate with the video's content.

This not only enhances viewer engagement but can also be a subtle avenue for monetization.

Introducing emojis in your description can add a touch of vibrancy and fun. These tiny symbols can be both visually appealing and functional. For instance, placing a link emoji next to a product link or a book emoji before a promotional link for a book can make the description more interactive and intuitive. It's a small touch, but one that can make your description stand out in a sea of plain text.

When crafting your description, there's a general structure that can amplify its effectiveness. Start with the title of the video. This isn't just repetition; it's a nod to the algorithm, ensuring it understands the core of your content. Following the title, place the most crucial link you want to highlight. Remember, moderation is key. Flooding your description with numerous links can come off as insincere and overly promotional. Aim for one to three pertinent links. Then, delve into a more detailed video description, painting a clearer picture of what viewers can expect. Conclude with three well-researched hashtags. These should be relevant to your video's theme and ideally, ones that are trending or have a high search volume.

In essence, a well-crafted description is like a roadmap, guiding viewers through your content and pointing them to additional treasures. It's an art, blending strategy with genuine information, and when done right, it can significantly elevate your YouTube game

To illustrate, consider these examples:

Example 1:

SIGMA Male Revenge: What Happens When They're Pushed Too Far (2023)

Connect With Sigma Males:
https://thesigmahub.com

YouTube Link:
https://www.youtube.com/watch?v=laEHX5kBDgl

Blog:
https://medium.com/@motivatorexpress/sigma-males-the-sinister-shift-when-betrayed-a1f39b4f63fd

Ever wondered what happens when a sigma male feels wronged? This video delves into the transformation of the calm, nurturing sigma into a strategic force to be reckoned with.

#sigmamale #sigma #sigmarule

Example 2:

5 Incredible AI Tools Which Will Make You Money (2023)

The Latest AI Projects:
https://aihackss.com

Blog:
https://medium.com/@motivatorexpress/unleashing-creativity-ai-blog-writing-with-writesonic-b3c31c5b2996

Dive into 2023's top AI tools set to skyrocket your earnings! Explore how Artificial Intelligence is reshaping financial strategies and uncover 5 game-changing tools that promise lucrative returns. Perfect for entrepreneurs, investors, or tech enthusiasts eager to capitalize on the AI revolution. Like, share, and subscribe for the latest in tech profitability!

#ai #makemoney #artificialintelligence

Tags, in the YouTube context, are not the same as the hashtags you might include in your video description. When you're in the process of uploading a video, you'll encounter a dedicated section specifically for tags. This is separate from the description box, and it's crucial not to conflate the two. While both serve the purpose of categorizing and providing context, they operate differently within the platform's framework.

For those just starting, it might be tempting to flood this section with numerous tags, hoping to cast a wide net. However, less is often more. A focused approach, using around 6-8 well-chosen tags, is generally optimal. These tags should be laser-focused on your content's essence, reflecting the primary themes and subjects of your video.

It's worth noting that the weightage of tags in YouTube's algorithm has evolved over time. While they once held significant sway in determining video rankings, their influence has diminished. But that doesn't render them obsolete. On the contrary, they still play a role, albeit a more nuanced one. Tags can act as subtle signposts, guiding viewers towards content that aligns with their interests.

In essence, while tags might not be the powerhouse they once were, they remain a valuable tool in your YouTube toolkit. By ensuring they're relevant and reflective of your content, you're giving your videos an added layer of context, enhancing discoverability in an ever-expanding digital landscape.

Chapter 5: Monetization Basics

Disclaimer: All comments and suggestions related to monetization within this book are provided as advice and general information. It is essential for readers to conduct their own thorough research and consult with a trained accountant or financial advisor regarding tax implications and other financial matters specific to their individual circumstances. The author and publisher are not responsible for any financial decisions or actions taken based on the content of this book. Always seek professional guidance when it comes to your unique financial situation.

One of the most significant milestones for budding YouTubers is reaching the 1,000 subscriber mark. But why is this number so crucial? Achieving 1,000 subscribers is one of the eligibility criteria for the YouTube Partner Program, a gateway to monetizing your channel through ads and fan support.

However, subscribers alone aren't the only metric YouTube considers. Alongside this, there's another crucial benchmark: accumulating 4,000 hours of watch time or garnering 10 million public Shorts views. These metrics ensure that channels have a consistent viewership and are producing content that engages audiences.

The YouTube Partner Program is a game-changer for creators. It's YouTube's way of recognizing and rewarding content creators for their hard work. Once you're part of this program, advertisements can be displayed on your videos, allowing you to earn revenue. But to be considered for this esteemed program, there are specific criteria to meet. Beyond the 1,000 subscribers, your channel needs to have garnered 4,000 valid public watch hours over the past year.

Achieving these milestones isn't just about the numbers; it's about the recognition of your dedication to content creation. It's a testament to the time and effort you've invested in connecting with your audience and delivering content that resonates. As you inch closer to these milestones, remember that they are more than just prerequisites for monetization. They symbolize your growth as a creator, your connection with your audience, and the promising potential of what lies ahead in your YouTube career.

Achieving swift monetization is no small feat, and it demands more than just passion—it requires dedication, perseverance, and an unwavering work ethic.

My journey stands as a clear example of this dedication. To monetize a niche channel in just 28 days, I fully immersed myself in my work, often sacrificing social outings and leisure time. Each evening, I dedicated 4-5 hours, deeply engrossed in creating content, refining my skills, and ensuring that every video was better than the previous one. While many creators might be tempted to spread their promotional efforts across different platforms, my focus remained unwavering. My growth was driven not by external promotions but by the consistent and high-quality content I consistently uploaded to my channel.

But what does consistency truly mean in the YouTube context? It's not just about posting frequently, but also about establishing a rhythm—a predictable pattern that viewers can rely on. Uploading 2-4 times a week, preferably on the same days and around the same times, can work wonders. It's akin to how popular TV series air episodes at consistent times on specific days. Viewers, over time, become accustomed to this schedule, eagerly anticipating the next installment. This predictability fosters loyalty, with audiences more likely to return, knowing exactly when to expect fresh content.

However, consistency in posting is just one piece of the puzzle. As highlighted in Chapter 4, the professionalism of your content elements—be it titles, descriptions, or thumbnails—plays a pivotal role in capturing and retaining viewer attention. When these elements are polished and aligned with your consistent posting schedule, it creates a synergy that not only boosts viewer engagement but also accelerates the path to monetization.

In essence, while the allure of YouTube success might seem enticing, the path is paved with dedication and hard work. But for those willing to commit, to post consistently, and to ensure every aspect of their content shines, the rewards—both in terms of audience loyalty and monetization—are well within reach.

Upon achieving monetization, the immediate subsequent step is to configure your AdSense for the purpose of monetization. AdSense is the gateway through which YouTube creators receive their earnings. Thus, having an active AdSense account becomes indispensable to access your YouTube revenue.

To initiate, if you're not already equipped with an AdSense account, you'll need to set one up via YouTube Studio. Detailed guidelines have been curated to assist you in this process, ensuring you navigate any common challenges with ease. It's pivotal to note that AdSense's Terms and Conditions permit only one account under a singular payee name. Therefore, it's crucial to ensure there aren't any duplicate accounts associated with your YouTube channel. If your intention is merely to modify the AdSense account linked to your channel, there's a straightforward procedure to follow.

Post the account setup, the next phase involves verifying your personal details. AdSense will dispatch a Personal Identification Number (PIN) to your registered address once your earnings surpass the address verification threshold. This PIN is crucial as it's required to authenticate your address prior to any payouts. Furthermore, based on your geographical location, there might be a necessity to validate your identity using specifics like your name, address, or date of birth.

Tax-related information is another crucial component. Google retains US taxes on earnings generated from US viewers. Hence, it's imperative to furnish this information to determine the accurate withholding rate. Once your personal and tax details are in place, the next milestone is to select a payment method. This becomes relevant once your earnings reach the payment method selection threshold.

Your finalized YouTube earnings for each month are credited to your AdSense account between the 7th and 12th of the succeeding month. Post this, the payment details, inclusive of any tax deductions, can be accessed on the Transactions page. Typically, if all conditions are met, payments are processed between the 21st and 26th of each month.

For those looking to establish a new AdSense account and link it to their channel, the procedure is straightforward. Begin by signing into YouTube Studio and selecting the Earn tab. From there, the on-screen prompts will guide you through the process, from re-authenticating your YouTube account to selecting the desired Google Account for AdSense. Once your application is submitted, AdSense will review it, a process that might span several days. Upon approval, a confirmation will be visible within YouTube Studio, indicating that your AdSense account is active and approved.

Understanding how YouTube monetization works is crucial. For those new to this platform, monetization is the process by which creators earn money from their videos, primarily through advertisements. To get a clear picture of how earnings are calculated, it's vital to familiarize oneself with two key terms: CPM and RPM.

Let's break it down. CPM, which stands for Cost Per Mille, indicates the amount advertisers are ready to pay for every 1,000 times their advertisement appears on a video. But here's the catch: this amount is calculated before YouTube takes its portion of the earnings. On the flip side, RPM, short for Revenue Per Mille, tells creators how much they will actually earn for every 1,000 views of their video, after YouTube has taken its share. Think of CPM as the gross amount and RPM as the net amount that lands in a creator's pocket.

Now, it's common for newcomers to get a tad confused between CPM and RPM. Here's a simple way to look at it: Advertisers focus on CPM because it tells them their advertising costs, while creators should keep an eye on RPM, as it reveals their actual earnings after all deductions.

So, what's a good RPM for a creator? While it can vary, on average, an RPM value between $3.30 and $4.40 is considered standard. This is in line with the CPM values in the US, which usually fall between $6 and $8. If a creator's RPM is around $3, they're on the right track. But remember, these are just averages. The actual figures can differ based on the video's topic. For example, videos about topics like personal finance, health, or makeup might have a higher CPM because advertisers value these audiences more.

One question that often pops up is: How much does YouTube pay for views? On average, for every view, a creator might earn about $0.018. So, if a video gets 1,000 views, that's roughly $18 in earnings. But, of course, this is just an average, and actual earnings can vary.

In conclusion, as creators embark on their YouTube journey, understanding these financial metrics is essential. With the right knowledge and a commitment to producing quality content, success on this platform is not just a dream but a very achievable reality.

Chapter 6: Advanced Monetization Strategies

Disclaimer: All comments and suggestions related to monetization within this book are provided as advice and general information. It is essential for readers to conduct their own thorough research and consult with a trained accountant or financial advisor regarding tax implications and other financial matters specific to their individual circumstances. The author and publisher are not responsible for any financial decisions or actions taken based on the content of this book. Always seek professional guidance when it comes to your unique financial situation.

Beyond the realm of ad revenues lies a potent strategy that many seasoned creators harness to boost their income: Affiliate Marketing. Let's delve into this lucrative avenue.

Affiliate marketing, in its essence, is a performance-based marketing strategy where creators promote products or services and earn a commission for every sale made through their referral. Think of it as being a digital ambassador for a product or service, and in return, you get a slice of the profit for every successful transaction that originated from your promotion.

For those wondering how to get started, it's simpler than it might seem. A quick search on Google for 'affiliate marketing programs' can unveil a plethora of opportunities tailored to various niches. Let's say a creator's content revolves around website design and HTML tutorials. In such a scenario, they could partner with a company like Softr, which offers user-friendly website design solutions. By promoting a unique link, such as "https://softrplatformsgmbh.grsm.io/softr5578", the "/softr5578" at the end acts as a tracker. It signals to Softr that the visitor arrived at their platform via that specific creator's referral. If the visitor decides to avail of Softr's services and makes a payment, the creator earns a commission. It's worth noting that commission rates can differ widely among companies, ranging anywhere from 5% to a whopping 50%.

Now, having this affiliate link is one thing, but positioning it effectively is another. A proven method is to place the link in the video description, making it easily accessible for viewers. But for those who want to ensure maximum visibility, pinning the link as the top comment is a brilliant move. Simply write a comment containing the affiliate link, click on the three dots next to the comment, and choose the 'pin' option. This ensures that the comment remains at the top, offering every viewer immediate access to the link.

Communication with one's audience is paramount, especially when integrating affiliate marketing into one's content strategy. A genuine and friendly approach can make all the difference. During the video, creators can take a brief moment to verbally inform their viewers about the affiliate link. A simple mention, such as "Hey, if you're interested in the product I've been talking about, I've dropped a link in the description and also pinned it in the comments for easy access," can be incredibly effective. It's also a good practice to add a touch of transparency by letting viewers know that by using the provided link, they're directly supporting the growth and sustainability of the channel. This not only fosters trust but also strengthens the bond between the creator and their audience. After all, viewers are more likely to support creators when they feel a genuine connection and understand that their actions, even as simple as clicking on a link, can have a positive impact on the channel they love.

Affiliate marketing can serve as a powerful tool in a creator's monetization arsenal. By aligning with products and services that resonate with their content and audience, creators can not only offer added value to their viewers but also enjoy a steady stream of additional income.

Following on from affiliate marketing, it's essential to understand another powerful monetization avenue: sponsored content. While both affiliate marketing and sponsored content involve collaborations between creators and brands, there are distinct differences and similarities between the two.

Affiliate marketing primarily revolves around promoting products or services and earning a commission for every sale made through a creator's unique link. The creator's earnings are directly tied to the audience's actions, whether it's clicking on a link or making a purchase. In contrast, sponsored content involves a brand compensating a creator upfront to integrate their product or message into a video. The creator's earnings are not dependent on the number of sales or clicks but rather on the agreement made with the brand.

However, the common thread between the two is the emphasis on genuine and authentic promotion. In both scenarios, the most successful collaborations arise when the product or brand aligns seamlessly with the creator's content and audience. This ensures that the promotion feels natural and resonates with viewers, rather than coming off as a forced advertisement.

For those unfamiliar, imagine watching a video where the creator pauses to discuss a product, perhaps demonstrating its use or sharing personal experiences with it. This could be a tech enthusiast unboxing the latest gadget, a gamer showcasing a new release, or a beauty influencer trying out a new skincare product. The essence of this strategy is to intertwine the brand's message seamlessly within the creator's content, making it relatable and genuine.

However, for this strategy to be effective, there needs to be a synergy between the creator's content and the brand's values.

It's not just about showcasing a product; it's about aligning with a brand that resonates with the creator's audience. This alignment ensures that the content feels authentic and not forced. After all, viewers are savvy and can easily discern when a creator is genuinely passionate about a product versus when they're merely promoting it for monetary gains.

Now, let's address a question that's likely on the minds of many budding YouTubers: How much can one earn from these brand deals? The answer, as with many things in the digital space, varies. Brands consider several factors when determining compensation, such as the creator's audience size, engagement rate, and content niche. For instance, a channel with an average of 50,000 to 100,000 views might command anywhere from $5,000 to $8,000 for a sponsored video. However, these figures can fluctuate based on the brand's budget, the creator's negotiation skills, and the perceived value of the collaboration.

For those unsure about pricing their sponsored content, a general guideline is to estimate the potential views a video might garner and then charge brands $20 to $30 for every thousand views. This approach provides a ballpark figure, but remember, the true value of a collaboration goes beyond mere numbers. It's about the quality of engagement, the fit between the brand and the creator, and the potential for long-term partnerships.

So, how does one land these coveted brand deals? Networking plays a pivotal role. Building relationships with fellow creators, engaging with brands on social media, and attending industry events can open doors to potential collaborations. For those who prefer a more structured approach, platforms like Artbrief, Scrunch, and Makrwatch connect creators with brands looking for partnerships. These platforms streamline the process, making it easier for creators to find suitable brand deals.

However, always remember to read the terms and conditions before committing to any platform or deal. Some platforms might have prerequisites, like a minimum subscriber count, while others might take a commission from the deal.

Lastly, YouTube itself offers a service called BrandConnect, designed to bridge the gap between creators and brands. This platform, formerly known as FameBit, aids creators in finding brand partnerships while providing brands with valuable insights and tools to measure their campaign's effectiveness.

Sponsored content offers a lucrative avenue for creators to monetize their content while providing value to brands. However, the key to successful brand collaborations lies in authenticity, alignment of values, and open communication. As creators venture into the realm of sponsored content, it's essential to remain true to one's brand and audience, ensuring that every collaboration feels genuine and adds value to the viewer's experience.

YouTube, merchandising has emerged as a promising avenue for creators to bolster their income. While the concept of selling merchandise related to one's channel isn't new, YouTube's recent initiatives have made it even more accessible for creators to sell directly from within their channels.

Merchandising, in essence, allows creators to design and sell products like t-shirts, mugs, and other items that resonate with their brand and content. This not only provides fans with tangible tokens of their favorite channels but also offers creators an additional revenue stream. Many seasoned YouTubers have recognized that solely depending on traditional YouTube revenue might not be sustainable in the long run. Hence, diversifying income through merchandise sales can be both lucrative and stabilizing. For some, it might even evolve into their primary source of income over time.

So, how does one get started with merchandising on YouTube? Here's a simplified guide:

Firstly, creators can set up an account on platforms like Printful who practically ship items worldwide. This platform allows them to seamlessly integrate their unique logos and designs onto a variety of products, from apparel to accessories. Once the designs are ready, the next step involves setting up an online storefront. Shopify is a popular choice for this purpose. After creating a Shopify account, products from Printful can be imported directly to the Shopify store. Shopify then takes on the role of processing customer payments, managing invoices, and listing products for sale.

The final step is to integrate the Shopify store with the YouTube channel. This ensures that fans can easily access and purchase merchandise directly while watching videos. The process is straightforward: when a customer places an order, Shopify handles the payment and notifies the creator. Simultaneously, Printful gets the cue to produce the ordered item. For instance, if a product is sold for $15, Shopify processes the payment and credits the creator. Printful then charges, say $7, for producing and shipping the item to the customer. The creator's profit, in this case, would be $8, which would be subject to applicable taxes.

YouTube, channel memberships stand out as another distinctive strategy, enabling creators to build a more profound relationship with their dedicated viewers. This feature allows enthusiasts of a particular channel to elevate their status from mere viewers to esteemed members. By embracing this membership, they agree to a monthly subscription, which, in return, unlocks a suite of exclusive benefits tailored just for them.

These exclusive benefits, often termed 'perks', can encompass a variety of offerings. From unique badges that distinguish them in the bustling comment sections to custom emojis that amplify their interactions, the possibilities are vast. But the essence of channel memberships extends beyond these. Creators can further captivate their members with access to videos reserved solely for them, live chat sessions that offer a more intimate interaction, and a plethora of other content designed exclusively for this inner circle. The versatility of channel memberships is truly its strength. Creators hold the reins, determining the structure of membership levels and the corresponding rewards, ensuring a bespoke experience that resonates with their audience's desires and aspirations.

The introduction of channel memberships not only carves out an additional avenue for revenue but also fosters a tighter-knit community. By curating these member-only experiences, creators can nurture a deeper sense of community and loyalty, fortifying the bond they share with their most passionate supporters.

Where creators and fans constantly seek innovative ways to interact, two features have emerged as game-changers in the realm of live streams and Premieres: Super Chat and Super Stickers. These tools are designed to amplify the voice of the viewer, allowing them to stand out amidst the bustling crowd of comments and interactions.

Super Chat is a unique offering that empowers viewers to purchase a special message during a live stream or Premiere. This purchased message is then prominently highlighted within the live chat, ensuring that it captures the creator's attention amidst the sea of comments. It's a direct bridge between the fan and the creator, allowing for a moment of recognition and connection.

On the other hand, Super Stickers offer a more visual form of interaction. Instead of just text, viewers can buy animated images that pop up in the live chat. These vibrant animations not only add a touch of fun and flair to the conversation but also serve as a distinctive way for fans to express their support and enthusiasm.

Both these features underscore the evolving nature of creator-fan interactions on YouTube. They not only provide an additional revenue stream for creators but also enrich the live streaming experience, making it more interactive, engaging, and memorable for all involved.

Chapter 7: YouTube Shorts and Reels

YouTube has introduced a new feature that's gaining popularity: YouTube Shorts. In this chapter, we'll explore what YouTube Shorts are and why they're becoming a favorite. Simply put, YouTube Shorts are short videos, no longer than 60 seconds, designed for quick viewing. They're easy to make, without the need for fancy equipment, giving creators a chance to be creative and connect with their audience in a new way.

Often, creators add a brief description to their Shorts. This description gives viewers an idea of what the video is about, helping them decide if they want to watch it.

Today, everything is fast-paced. From quick food deliveries to instant rides with apps like Uber, people want things now. This fast pace has shortened our attention spans, especially among younger viewers. They prefer quick, engaging content. As the online world keeps changing, creators need to adapt and offer content that fits these changing preferences.

For YouTube Shorts, the message is simple: make it short and make it count. If a creator's audience prefers longer videos, it's essential to keep that in mind. Mixing long videos with Shorts can confuse subscribers. Instead, creators should focus on making impactful Shorts that grab attention right away.

Starting with a captivating hook is essential, but it's just the tip of the iceberg. To truly captivate your audience, consider re-engaging them every few seconds. This can be achieved by incorporating popular sounds, intriguing text overlays, or striking visuals. The key is to keep the momentum going, ensuring that every moment of the Short is as engaging as the first.

Being in tune with the pulse of the digital world is crucial. Familiarize yourself with the latest trends, challenges, and viral sensations. By aligning your content with what's currently popular, you enhance the chances of your Shorts gaining traction and resonating with a broader audience. Moreover, consistency is your ally. By establishing a regular posting rhythm, you give your audience something to anticipate, fostering a sense of loyalty and eagerness for your next creation.

When considering best practices for YouTube Shorts, regular posting stands out. Given the emphasis YouTube places on new features, it's plausible that Shorts are being prioritized in terms of performance metrics. This makes it all the more essential to maintain a steady flow of content. Additionally, captions can be a game-changer. They offer an additional layer of engagement, allowing you to communicate more effectively with your viewers. Incorporating trending music, relevant hashtags, and current events can further amplify your Shorts' reach.

But beyond the trends and tactics, the essence of a compelling Short lies in its ability to evoke curiosity. Understand your audience's preferences and craft content that resonates with them. Visual appeal is paramount; vibrant and unique visuals can make your content stand out in a sea of Shorts. Moreover, even within the constraints of a Short, storytelling can be a powerful tool. Weaving a narrative, no matter how brief, can make your content more relatable and memorable. Lastly, for content that truly strikes a chord, consider integrating elements of ethos, pathos, and logos. These age-old rhetorical devices can add depth and persuasion to your Shorts, making them not just watchable, but unforgettable.

First and foremost, the key to monetizing Shorts lies within the platform's monetization tab. This section provides a comprehensive overview of the various avenues available for creators to earn from their content. For those who've already ventured into the earlier chapters on monetization, it might be beneficial to revisit those sections. They offer a wealth of knowledge that can be applied directly to the world of Shorts.

Affiliate marketing stands out as a potent method for monetization. By promoting products or services within your Shorts and earning a commission for every sale made through your referral, you can create a steady stream of income. The beauty of affiliate marketing is its versatility; it can be seamlessly integrated into any content type, including Shorts.

However, the crown jewel of monetization on YouTube is undoubtedly the YouTube Partner Program (YPP). By becoming a member of this program, creators unlock a treasure trove of monetization tools. Not only can you place ads on your videos, but you also gain the opportunity to directly monetize your audience. This could be through fan-funding or other direct support mechanisms that YouTube offers. In essence, while Shorts are brief in duration, their potential to generate revenue is vast. With the right strategies and a touch of creativity, Shorts can become a lucrative addition to any creator's content portfolio.

The YouTube Shorts algorithm, in its essence, functions by analyzing user behavior and video topics to anticipate the kind of content a viewer might be inclined to watch next.

Interestingly, there was a time when the regular YouTube algorithm and the Shorts algorithm operated independently. However, a pivotal change occurred in August 2022. The platform began integrating a viewer's Shorts viewing history into its recommendations for long-form content. This integration underscores the growing importance of Shorts in the broader YouTube ecosystem.

For those aiming to maximize their reach through YouTube Shorts, a balanced approach is recommended. While Shorts can be a fantastic tool to attract a new audience, it's equally vital to offer regular video content. The synergy between Shorts and standard videos can be powerful. Shorts can act as a magnet, drawing viewers to explore more in-depth content on your channel, and conversely, your regular videos can pique interest in your Shorts, creating a harmonious cycle of engagement.

When crafting a Short, the initial moments are crucial. Capturing a viewer's attention right from the outset is paramount. Experimentation is key here. Play around with various techniques and strategies to ensure your audience remains glued to the screen till the very last second.

For those with aspirations of rapid growth and dreams of their content going viral, frequency is your ally. Posting two to three Shorts daily can significantly amplify your chances of achieving these goals. However, for smaller creators, this might seem like a daunting task. But remember, every journey begins with a single step. Start with what's manageable and gradually build your momentum. The world of YouTube Shorts is vast, and with dedication and creativity, the sky's the limit.

Chapter 8: Faceless Channels

There's a distinctive category that's been gaining traction: Faceless Channels. As we dive into this chapter, let's uncover the essence of this intriguing concept.

At its core, a faceless YouTube channel is one where the creator remains unseen. Instead of personal appearances, these channels often feature stock videos, various footage, or even recordings from computer or phone screens. The identity of the creator, including their face and sometimes even their real voice, remains concealed. The focus shifts from the individual behind the camera to the content being presented.

Such channels offer a fresh perspective on content creation. By removing the personal element, they open up a realm of possibilities for those who might be camera-shy or simply prefer to keep their identity private. But the benefits don't stop at anonymity. Faceless channels present a canvas ripe for innovation, allowing creators to experiment with diverse content forms without the constraints of personal branding.

Drawing inspiration from seasoned professionals in this space, it becomes evident that faceless channels aren't just a fleeting trend. They represent a viable avenue for growth, artistic expression, and potentially lucrative returns. For those willing to explore this path, the potential rewards, both creatively and financially, can be significant.

A popular choice for many faceless channels is making tutorials. For example, you could teach people how to use Photoshop, how to use different software, or even how to play certain video games. But remember, if you're showing content from games or software, you need to make sure you're allowed to use it, especially if you want to make money from your videos. It's always a good idea to check the rules first. You can usually find this information with a quick online search.

Another great idea for content is using stock videos. These are ready-made videos that you can put together to tell a story or explain a topic. You can talk over these videos or, if you're not comfortable with that, there are software options that can create voice-overs for you. There are many places online, like Adobe CC, Clipchamp, and Flexclip, where you can find these stock videos.

Many stock video websites operate on a subscription model, charging creators a monthly fee. In return, they provide access to a vast library of videos that can be used in your projects. The advantage here is that these platforms often come with licenses that allow you to not only use the videos but also to monetize them on platforms like YouTube. This means that while there's an upfront cost, the potential returns from a successful video can make it a worthwhile investment.

Moreover, the evolution of technology has brought forth advanced AI software that can be a game-changer for faceless channels. Some of these software solutions offer comprehensive packages, taking care of both video editing and voice-over needs. Imagine having a tool that not only provides the visuals but also narrates your content, all powered by artificial intelligence. This seamless integration can save time, effort, and even money in the long run. For those curious about how these AI tools work and their potential benefits, stay tuned. The upcoming chapter will delve deeper into this fascinating topic, equipping you with knowledge to elevate your content creation journey.

Now, you might be wondering what kind of stories or topics you can cover with stock videos. Well, there are so many options! You could make videos about interesting facts about animals, or dive into topics like psychology and different personality types. Health tips, explanations about how love works, or even mysteries like UFOs and ancient civilizations like Egypt are all great topics. The main thing is to pick something you're interested in and think others will be too.

In the end, faceless channels offer a lot of freedom. You don't have to be on camera, but you can still share your ideas, stories, and knowledge with the world. With a bit of creativity and research, you can make content that people will love to watch.

One of the most effective ways to monetize faceless channels is through affiliate marketing. By promoting products or services within your videos, you can earn a commission for every sale made through your referral link. This method can be particularly lucrative if the products or services align well with the content of your videos and the interests of your audience.

In addition to affiliate marketing, selling merchandise can also be a profitable avenue. Imagine creating themed merchandise that resonates with the content of your videos. Even without showing your face, your channel's brand can have a strong identity, and fans might be eager to purchase items that connect them more deeply to your content.

Of course, ad revenue remains a staple for most YouTubers, faceless channels included. As your channel grows and attracts more views, the revenue from ads can become a significant income stream.

For a deeper dive into affiliate marketing, merchandise sales, and other monetization strategies, chapters 5 and 6 of this book offer in depth insights. By combining the knowledge from those chapters with the unique nature of faceless channels, you can craft a monetization strategy that's both effective and tailored to your content.

While the allure of faceless channels lies in their anonymity and the freedom they offer, it's essential to tread carefully and ensure that all content respects the legal rights of others.

First and foremost, copyright is a significant concern. Even if you're not showing your face, the visuals and audio you use must either be original, licensed, or fall under the category of fair use. For instance, using stock footage is common in faceless channels, but always ensure you have the right licenses to use and monetize such content. Unauthorized use can lead to strikes against your channel, potential legal action, and loss of revenue.

Voiceovers, whether they're your own or generated through software, should also be original. Avoid using copyrighted music or sound effects without proper permissions. If you're commenting on or reviewing copyrighted content, ensure you're doing so in a way that could be considered fair use, though this can be a gray area and might vary by jurisdiction.

Privacy is another crucial aspect. Even if you're not revealing your identity, ensure you're not inadvertently disclosing someone else's private information or using content that invades another person's privacy.

Lastly, if you're promoting products, services, or even conducting affiliate marketing, transparency is key. It's a good practice, and often a legal requirement, to disclose any affiliations or sponsorships to your audience.

In conclusion, while faceless channels offer a unique and exciting avenue for content creation on YouTube, they come with their own set of legal considerations. Being informed and cautious can help ensure your channel's longevity and success without unwanted legal complications. Always consider consulting with a legal professional if you're unsure about any aspects of your content.

Chapter 9: AI Power: Advanced Faceless Channel Strategies

Artificial Intelligence (AI) stands as a revolutionary force, reshaping the way content is conceived, crafted, and delivered. The advent of AI has ushered in a new era where content creation is not only faster but also more efficient when harnessed correctly.

AI's prowess extends beyond just video creation. It plays a pivotal role in optimizing search engine results, crafting compelling titles, and formulating descriptions that captivate and draw viewers in. The potential of AI in these domains is immense, and when utilized effectively, it can significantly elevate the quality and reach of your content.

As we delve deeper into this chapter, we'll explore strategic methods to produce AI-driven videos in a cost-effective manner. While leveraging AI does come with a price tag, the investment is often justified by the exponential increase in content creation speed, sometimes amplifying the pace by 30 to 50 times. This acceleration allows creators to churn out high-quality content at a rate previously deemed unattainable.

However, it's essential to tread with caution. While tools like ChatGPT offer immense potential, we'll be steering clear of them in this discussion due to potential copyright concerns. That said, for those familiar with its features, ChatGPT can be a valuable asset, especially when prompted correctly. The key lies in understanding its capabilities and harnessing them in a manner that aligns with one's content goals and vision.

AI is not just a tool; it's a transformative force in the world of YouTube content creation. By embracing its capabilities and understanding its features, creators can unlock a world of

63

possibilities, setting their channels apart in an increasingly competitive digital space.

Now, if you're interested in trying out this AI magic for your channel, there are two main websites you should know about. If you've heard of ChatGPT and are using it, you'll want to pay special attention to the second website we'll mention. To get started with these sites, you can either scan the QR codes we've provided or just click on the links we've shared. Both ways will lead you to set up trial accounts for free.

The first QR code will take you to a website that's all about helping you write scripts for your videos. Think of it as having a smart writer by your side, suggesting what to say in your videos. This AI-powered tool can come up with interesting and engaging stories or information that your viewers will love.

QR CODE 1
https://bit.ly/youtubetexts

The second QR code is designed especially for those who've already crafted their scripts and are now at the stage of bringing their vision to life through video. Once you input your script into this innovative platform, the AI takes over, acting as your personal video editor. Not only will it select fitting videos, but it will also curate the perfect background music, and if needed, provide voiceovers that harmonize with your content. Imagine having a seasoned film director and editor at your fingertips, guiding you on the best visual choices to complement your narrative. What's truly remarkable is the AI's precision in selecting video clips that align with your script's tone and content. This ensures that the end product isn't just another video but a polished, captivating piece that holds your viewers' interest from start to finish.

QR CODE 2
https://bit.ly/Youtubestockvideo

To sum it up, using AI tools can make the whole process of creating YouTube videos smoother and more professional. It's like having a team of experts, from writers to directors, helping you out. By taking advantage of these tools, you're giving your YouTube channel a big boost, making it stand out in a sea of content.

One of the best AI tools out there for YouTube creators if used correctly is ChatGPT. It's like having a smart helper by your side, especially when you're trying to think of what to name your video or what to write in the video's description.

Why are titles and descriptions so important? Well, think about when you're scrolling through YouTube. The first thing you see is the video's title. If it sounds interesting, you might click on it. The description then gives you a bit more info about what the video is about. So, having a catchy title and a clear description can really help get more people to watch your videos. If you need to familiarize yourself with titles and descriptions, I suggest reading chapter 4 again.

Now, let's talk about how to use ChatGPT to help with this. The key is to ask it in the right way. You give it some information about your video, and it gives you back a title or description idea. It's like asking a friend for advice, but this friend is powered by AI!

Here are some example prompts to give you an idea:

"Hey ChatGPT, my video is about easy cooking tips for college students. Can you suggest a title that would make students want to click?"

"ChatGPT, I've made a fun video about training puppies. What's a catchy title and description idea?"

"I need a title, ChatGPT! My video is about DIY crafts using recycled materials. Any ideas?"

"ChatGPT, help me out. I've filmed a workout routine for busy parents. What should I name it?"

"I've got a video about traveling on a budget in Europe. Can you think of a title and description that would attract backpackers?"

By using prompts like these, you can get AI to help you come up with titles and descriptions that really stand out. Remember, on YouTube, it's all about grabbing attention, and with ChatGPT by your side, you've got a better chance of doing just that.

A more interesting and in-depth prompt:

Hello CHAT GPT,

I am my next YouTube video based on the topic of '10 ways to make money online'.

Please can you write me an enhanced keyword rich, and SEO optimised:
1. High click through rate YouTube title
2. Engaging and well-read YouTube description
3. Relevant YouTube tags

I would also like you to write a YouTube script for the above

Make sure the text is keyword rich and optimised for YouTube and googles search engines.

Research and use 'make money online/passive income/working from home/how to make money on the internet' related keywords and relatable long tail keywords to help with YouTube and googles algorithm Use the CHAT GPT 4 keyword plugin to find what money-making keywords will work with this particular video. Make it all very rich in keywords.

The beginning needs to capture the reader's attention and start with the prominent title keywords in the first sentence.

I would like an introduction, 10 points and a conclusion.

Please write this text in 3rd person

Please write this text so it is; alluring, engaging, mysterious, factual, award winning, natural, human like and written as a professional blogger.

Please use correct grammar and punctuation.

Chapter 10: Social Media and Marketing Strategies

The next crucial step is ensuring that your content reaches the right audience. While YouTube's algorithm plays a significant role in this, there's a world outside of YouTube brimming with potential viewers. By leveraging the power of social media, you can organically boost your channel's visibility, which in turn, can positively influence YouTube's algorithm. Let's investigate some organic promotion strategies on various social media platforms.

Reddit and Quora: These platforms are goldmines for niche topics. Suppose your videos delve into the intriguing subject of dark psychology. In that case, you can scout for posts or questions related to themes like manipulation or mind games. Instead of blatantly promoting your video, craft a thoughtful response that adds value to the conversation. At the end of your detailed answer, you can subtly mention that you've explored this topic in one of your videos and share the link. This approach positions you as a helpful contributor rather than just another promoter.

Facebook: The world of Facebook groups offers a range of opportunities. Seek out groups that align with your content's niche. Engage in discussions, offer solutions, and share experiences. When it feels appropriate, you can reference one of your videos as a helpful resource. The key is to frame it in a way that it feels like a genuine recommendation at the end of helpful response rather than a self-promotion. For instance, saying, "I found this video helpful when I was learning about manipulation," feels more authentic than directly pushing your content.

Reddit, Quora and Facebook post and reply example:

Question:

How can I learn to be a manipulative person? How do manipulative people think? Can it be learned? Can it be perfected through exercise? What are the hallmarks of manipulative thinking? What characterizes a manipulator extraordinaire?

Reply:

Approaching the topic of manipulation with caution is essential, as using manipulative tactics in everyday relationships can be unethical and damaging. However, understanding how manipulative people operate can arm you against their tactics and help you protect yourself.

Understanding Manipulative Thinking:

1. Self-Centricity: *Manipulators often prioritize their needs, desires, and feelings above all else. They view situations primarily concerning their gains.*

***2.* Emotional Leverage:** *They are adept at identifying and exploiting people's emotional vulnerabilities. This can involve guilt-tripping, playing the victim, or gaslighting.*

3. Strategic Communication: *Manipulators often withhold information or share it selectively to create a narrative that benefits them.*

4. Feigning Innocence: *When confronted, they may feign ignorance or innocence, sometimes turning the tables to portray themselves as the victim.*

5. Consistency in Persuasion: *Manipulative individuals practice persistence in their persuasion attempts. They might wear someone down over time to get what they want.*

6. Flattery and Charm: *A manipulator may use excessive flattery to disarm others or make them more receptive to their demands.*

7. Avoidance of Accountability: *They rarely take responsibility for their actions and often shift the blame onto others.*

Learning and Perfecting:

While understanding these traits is beneficial to protect oneself, actively trying to adopt them can lead to negative outcomes in relationships, work, and personal well-being. Instead of trying to "learn" manipulation, it's better to focus on understanding these tactics to recognize and counteract them when you encounter them.

Remember, knowledge of manipulation should be used as a shield, not a sword. Being manipulative is not a trait to aspire to, but knowing how manipulators operate can help you protect yourself, especially if you find yourself frequently targeted by such individuals. It's always essential to approach interactions with empathy and genuine intention. If you're dealing with manipulators, stand firm in your boundaries and seek support when needed.

The below video has some great insights on manipulators, and I would recommend watching for further education:

(Enter Video Link)

Example Ending.

Medium: Medium holds a special place in my heart, and for a good reason. It's not just another place to pen down thoughts; it's a powerhouse for sustainable, organic growth. Let me explain why.

When you think of Medium, don't just see it as a blogging platform. Instead, envision it as a strategic ally in your content creation journey. If you've been diligently scripting your YouTube videos, you're sitting on a goldmine. Those scripts can be seamlessly transformed into comprehensive, engaging articles. This not only gives your content a second life but also reaches an audience that prefers reading over watching.

Now, to ensure your articles don't just get lost in the vast sea of content, it's essential to make them search-engine friendly. This is where AI tools come into play. Platforms like ChatGPT can be invaluable in crafting SEO-optimized titles and meta descriptions, ensuring that your content gets the visibility it deserves.

But why stop there? To enrich the reader's experience, embed your corresponding video at the end of the article. This multimedia approach caters to both readers and viewers, broadening your audience base.

One of Medium's standout features is its impressive domain authority. This means that with the right keywords and quality content, your articles have the potential to rank high on search engine results. And here's the best part: while comments or posts on platforms like Reddit or Facebook have a short lifespan, a well-crafted Medium article is timeless. It can consistently drive traffic, not just for days or weeks, but for years. Picture this: multiple articles, each drawing its own set of readers, all funneling into your YouTube channel. The potential for growth is immense.

In essence, Medium is more than just a platform; it's a tool, a strategy, and, if used correctly, a game-changer in your YouTube journey.

YouTube Ads: YouTube is a big place, and while many creators dream of growing their channels naturally, sometimes using paid ads can give your videos a big boost. Think of it like putting up a big sign in a busy area to let people know about your videos. One of the best tools for this is Google Ads.

Before we go deeper, let's clear up some confusion. There are two things here: Google Ads and AdSense. They might sound similar, but they're different. Google Ads is like a tool that lets you show your videos to more people. You can use it to promote your YouTube videos, your website, or even your whole channel. On the other side, AdSense is how you make money when other people show their ads on your videos. So, in simple words, Google Ads is for showing your ads, and AdSense is for making money from other people's ads.

Now, how can Google Ads help your YouTube channel? Well, one cool thing you can do is show your video before another popular video in your topic area. So, let's say someone wants to watch a video from a big YouTuber in your area. They click on that video, but before it starts, they see your video first. This is a great way to get your video in front of people who might like it.

To make this happen, you need to start by setting up a Google Ads account. Once you're in, you can make a special kind of ad that targets specific videos or channels. It's a way to make sure your video gets seen by the right people.

One of the most effective strategies before diving into paid advertising is to research other channels that align with your content theme. By studying these channels, you can identify trends, popular topics, and even the kind of audience they attract. Once you have a clear picture, you can strategically place your ads in front of their videos. This ensures that your content is presented to viewers who already have an interest in your niche. It's like setting up a stall at a market where everyone is already looking for what you offer. By targeting these channels with your ads, you're positioning your content right where it needs to be, maximizing the chances of drawing in an engaged and relevant audience.

This is really helpful if you're trying to tell people about a certain brand or product you have. By showing your video before a big YouTuber's video, you're not just getting more views. You're also reaching people who are already interested in your topic and might want to see more of your videos or buy your product.

To wrap it up, growing your channel naturally is great, but sometimes using tools like Google Ads can give you a big boost. It might cost some money, but if you do it right, it can help a lot. On YouTube, it's important to make good videos, but it's also important to make sure the right people see them.

Chapter 11: Analytics and Performance Metrics

YouTube success isn't just about creating compelling content; it's also about understanding how that content performs. YouTube Analytics is a treasure trove of data that provides insights into how viewers interact with your videos. By studying these metrics, creators can refine their strategies and optimize their content for better engagement and growth.

Traffic sources and ranking. Traffic sources reveal where your viewers are discovering your content. Are they stumbling upon your videos through YouTube search, external websites, or is it through suggested videos? On the other hand, "ranking" pertains to the position a video occupies in search results and its probability of appearing as a suggested video. Notably, on YouTube, suggested videos, which pop up in the right sidebar or at the conclusion of a video, stand as the premier traffic source. Grasping these concepts can significantly aid in tailoring your content and promotional strategies, ensuring you effectively reach your target audience.

Impressions and click-through rate (CTR) are important metrics in understanding viewer engagement.

So, what's an impression? Think of it as a first glance. Every time someone sees your video thumbnail, that's counted as one impression. It's like someone walking past a shop window and noticing a display.

Now, CTR is a bit different. It's all about action. Out of all the people who saw your video thumbnail (impressions), CTR tells you how many actually clicked on it to watch your video. It's a percentage, so if you have a CTR of 5%, that means out of every 100 people who saw your video thumbnail, 5 people clicked on it.

Why is this important? Well, if you've got a catchy video thumbnail and title, more people are likely to click on your video. And a higher CTR usually means you're on the right track. To give you a bit of context, many YouTube channels typically have a CTR between 2-10%. So, if you're hitting numbers within this range, you're doing pretty well. But if you're on the lower end, say around 2-3%, there might be some room to make your videos more click-worthy.

Remember, these numbers aren't set in stone. They can change based on what your video is about, who it's for, and how engaged your audience is. But the key takeaway is this: always aim to get that CTR higher. It's a good sign that your videos are grabbing attention and drawing viewers in.

Watch time and average view duration are key indicators of how well your content is resonating with viewers. Simply put, watch time is the total minutes people have spent watching your videos, and average view duration is how long, on average, they stick around for each video. These numbers tell you a lot about the appeal of your content.

Now, let's break it down a bit. If you're aiming for top performance, you'd ideally want your average view duration to be around 50 to 60% of the video's total length. So, if you've got a one-minute video, a good target would be for viewers to stay for at least 30 to 60 seconds. If they're sticking around for 70% or more of the video, you're doing exceptionally well!

However, context matters. For instance, in a tutorial video, viewers might jump straight to the specific step they need, skipping other parts. So, while a 7-minute average view duration on a 10-minute video is generally excellent, it can vary based on the video's content.

Another thing to note is audience retention after the first 30 seconds. If 70% of viewers are still with you after that initial half-minute, you're on the right track. A retention rate of 70-80% is even better, and anything above 80% is outstanding. High retention rates often mean that your video's title and thumbnail accurately represent the content, and the quality keeps viewers engaged.

Key moments for audience retention is a relatively newer metric that shows when viewers are most engaged or when they drop off. This can help you identify which parts of your video are most captivating or where improvements might be needed.

Engagement metrics like likes, dislikes, and comments on top videos provide a direct measure of how viewers are reacting to your content. Positive engagement can boost your video's visibility on the platform, while feedback in the form of comments can offer valuable insights for future content creation.

Understanding your audience's location, gender, age, and language can be instrumental in tailoring your content. For instance, if a significant portion of your audience comes from a particular country, you might consider adding subtitles in that language.

Metrics like returning viewers, unique viewers, and subscribers offer insights into your channel's growth and loyalty of your audience. Returning viewers indicate that your content is compelling enough for viewers to come back, while a rise in unique viewers can signal broader reach.

Watch time for subscribers tells you how engaged your subscribers are with your content. It's a measure of the total watch time from viewers who are subscribed to your channel. If this metric is high, it indicates that your core audience is actively consuming your content.

Understanding where your video traffic originates is a cornerstone of effective YouTube channel management. When you dive into your analytics, you'll notice a section labeled 'Traffic source types'. This provides a breakdown of where your viewers are coming from, and it's divided into two main categories: internal and external sources.

Internal traffic is generated from within the YouTube platform itself. This includes viewers discovering your content from the Home page, through their subscriptions, the Watch Later feature, Trending/Explore sections, and even from other YouTube channels. It's essentially traffic that originates from users already browsing the YouTube platform.

On the flip side, external traffic is what comes from outside of YouTube. This is where your promotional efforts on other platforms come into play. If you're active on social media platforms like Twitter, Facebook, or Instagram, or if you have an email list, these can be invaluable sources of traffic. Every time you release a new video, sharing it across these platforms can drive viewers to YouTube. Platforms like WhatsApp, Reddit, and even traffic from articles can contribute to this external traffic. YouTube values this kind of external engagement, as it indicates that your content is drawing viewers into their platform. In the world of YouTube analytics, every bit of traffic, whether it's from a tweet or a shared link in a WhatsApp group, plays a role in your video's ranking.

There's also a category of traffic labeled as 'unknown'. This might sound mysterious, but it's quite straightforward. Within YouTube Analytics, 'unknown' traffic is divided into direct and embedded. Direct traffic can encompass various sources, including bookmarks, mobile apps, and instances where tracking cookies aren't used. Embedded traffic, meanwhile, refers to views from your video when it's embedded on other websites or platforms. Both these types of unknown traffic are essential to consider, as they can represent a significant portion of your viewership.

In essence, understanding your traffic sources is like having a roadmap to your audience's behavior. It tells you where your viewers are coming from, which platforms are most effective for promotion, and where there might be opportunities for growth. By paying attention to these metrics, you can tailor your promotional strategies and content creation to better serve your audience and grow your channel.

Chapter 12: Delayed Gratification

Many people dream of quickly becoming famous on YouTube, imagining that one video will skyrocket them to stardom. However, experienced YouTubers often share a different story. They compare YouTube to a long race, like a marathon, rather than a short, fast sprint. Sure, every once in a while, a video might go viral and get a lot of attention. But most of the time, building a successful YouTube channel takes time and patience. It's about creating many videos, one after the other, and slowly growing your audience over months or even years. Just like constructing a building, it's done one brick at a time, with each video adding to the foundation of the channel's success.

Being consistent is like the secret sauce for a successful YouTube channel. Think of it like this: imagine your favorite TV show. You know it comes on at a certain time, on a certain day, every week. You look forward to it, and you make time for it. That's the kind of relationship you want with your YouTube audience. It doesn't mean you have to upload a new video every single day or even every week. What's important is setting a schedule that you can stick to, whether it's once a week, every other week, or even once a month.

When your viewers know when to expect new content from you, they're more likely to come back and watch. It's like making a promise to them, and each time you keep that promise by uploading when you said you would, you build trust. Over time, this trust turns casual viewers into loyal fans.

But there's another big reason to be consistent. YouTube has its own way of deciding which videos to show people, and it's called an algorithm. This algorithm likes channels that are active and regularly updated. So, by sticking to a schedule and consistently uploading, you're also telling YouTube that your channel is alive and kicking. This can help your videos get seen by even more people. In short, being consistent is a win-win: it's good for your viewers, and it's good for getting noticed on YouTube.

Having goals is like having a roadmap for your YouTube journey. It gives you direction and helps you know where you're headed. But just like when you're planning a trip, it's important to be realistic about how far you can go and how long it will take. Imagine wanting to drive from one city to another in just an hour when it's actually a five-hour journey. You'd end up feeling frustrated and tired, right? The same goes for your YouTube channel.

When you're just starting out, dreaming of having thousands of subscribers or millions of views is natural. After all, we often hear about viral videos and YouTube sensations. But aiming for such big numbers right away can be overwhelming. It's like trying to run a marathon without any training. You might end up feeling disappointed or, worse, so stressed that you want to give up.

Instead, think of your YouTube journey as a series of small steps. Maybe your first goal is to get your first 100 subscribers. Once you achieve that, aim for 500, and then maybe a thousand. Or perhaps you want to focus on views. Celebrate when your first video gets 100 views. Then, set a new goal, like reaching 500 views on your next video.

By setting smaller, more achievable goals, you give yourself the chance to celebrate little victories along the way. Each small win boosts your confidence and motivation. And over time, all these small achievements add up, helping you build a successful channel brick by brick. Remember, every big YouTuber started with just one subscriber and one view. It's the small steps, taken consistently, that lead to big success.

Lastly, while it's essential to live in the present and enjoy the journey, always keep an eye on the horizon. The digital landscape, especially platforms like YouTube, is ever-evolving. Stay informed about the latest trends, updates, and best practices. This proactive approach ensures that you're not just reacting to changes but are prepared for them, ensuring that your channel remains relevant and continues to thrive in the long run.

In conclusion, YouTube is not a platform for those seeking overnight success. It demands dedication, patience, and a strategic mindset. Embrace the journey, celebrate every milestone, and always remember: success on YouTube is a long game, and those who persevere are the ones who truly shine.

Printed in Great Britain
by Amazon